Quiet Moments with God

Maple Spring Publishing Titles

ORIGINAL CLASSIC EDITION

Quiet Moments with God

FEATURES BONUS BOOK: How to Use the Power of Prayer

JOSEPH MURPHY

MAPLE SPRING PUBLISHING

Published 2024 by Maple Spring Publishing

Front cover design by David Rheinhardt of Pyrographx

Interior design by Meghan Day Healey of Story Horse, LLC.

Library of Congress Cataloging-in-Publication Data is available upon request

ISBN: 979-8-3505-0076-9

10 9 8 7 6 5 4 3 2 1

Contents

Condensed Interpretation
of 23rd Psalm

❧·❧

The Lord is my shepherd. I sing the song of the jubilant soul for I have chosen God as my shepherd. Divine Intelligence rules and guides me in all my ways. I shall not want for peace, harmony, or guidance because God's Wisdom governs me. I lie down in green pastures always, since God is prospering me beyond my wildest dreams. I find myself beside the still waters as I claim the Infinite Peace of God floods my mind and heart. My emotions (waters) are stilled and calm. My mind is now serene and it reflects God's Heavenly Truths and Light (my soul is restored.) I think of God's Holy Presence within me all day long. I walk the path of righteousness through my devotion and attention to God's Eternal Verities. I know there is no death and I fear no evil. I know "God has not given us the spirit of fear, but of love and power, and a sound mind." God's rod (Love) and staff (Truth) comfort, sustain, and nourish me. The banquet table of God is always set before me; it is the Secret Place of the Most High, where in my thought I walk and talk with God. I eat the nourishing Truths of God whenever fear and worry (my enemies) trouble me. The bread I eat is God's idea of peace, love, and faith in all things good. The meat I eat is the Omnipotence of God; the wine I drink is the essence of joy. The Wisdom of God anoints my intellect; It is a Lamp unto my feet and a Light on my path. My cup (heart) is truly the chamber of God's Holy Presence; it runneth over with love and joy. I mentally dwell on Goodness, Truth, and Beauty; this is my House of God.

Condensed Interpretation of The 91st Psalm

I dwell in the Secret Place as I contemplate God and His Glory within me. I abide in the Shadow always because I know God's Love surrounds and enfolds me making straight, beautiful, and joyous my way. The Lord (The Spiritual Power) is Sovereign and Supreme, the Only Power. It responds to my thought; It is, therefore, my Refuge and my Fortress. This Spiritual Power inspires, heals, strengthens, and restores my mind and body. It is God. It is a Beneficent, Kindly Power. I trust It completely, and It responds as mercy, love, inspiration, and beauty. This Divine Power covers me with Its feathers of Love, Light, and Peace. It is wonderful!

I completely reject the negative thoughts of the world (the arrow by day), and God's Love dissolves the fear-patterns of my subconscious (terror by night). I know I am secure in the Invisible Hands of God. I always vibrate with the Mind of God and all is well. I am completely free from fear of accidents or hostile activities (pestilences that walketh in darkness) because I know I am immunized and God-intoxicated. I have received the Divine Anti-body—the Presence of God in my heart. The thousands of negative thoughts and suggestions of the world are destroyed consciously and subconsciously, for God walks and talks in me, and I live in the joyous expectancy of the best. (There shall no evil befall thee). God and His Holy Angels (God's Ideas, Impulses, Intuition, and Guidance) have complete charge over me, and I am safeguarded in all my ways—in health, right activity, self expression, and Divine companionship. By contemplating the Presence of God, I tread upon the lion and adder (obstacles and complexes of all kinds). My salvation (solution) is revealed to me as I think of God and Heaven; then all the Divine force hasten to minister to my eternal joy.

Healing Treatment

The gifts of God are mine. We are gathered together in the Presence of God from whom all blessings flow. I use every moment of this day to glorify God. God's Harmony, Peace, and Abundance are mine. Divine Love flowing from me blesses all who come into my atmosphere. God's Love is felt by all present here and His Love is healing them now.

I fear no evil for God is with me. I am always surrounded by the Sacred Circle of God's Love and Power. I claim, feel, know, and believe definitely and positively that the spell of God's Love and Eternal Watchfulness guides, heals, and takes care of all members of my family and loved ones.

I forgive everyone and I sincerely radiate God's Love, Peace, and Good will to all men everywhere. At the center of my being is Peace; this is the Peace of God. In this Stillness I feel His Strength, Guidance, and the Love of His Holy Presence. I am Divinely guided in all my ways. I am a clear channel for God's Love, Light, Truth, and Beauty. I feel His River of Peace flowing through me. I know that all my problems are dissolved in the Mind of God. God's ways are my ways. The words I have spoken accomplish that whereunto they are sent. I rejoice and give thanks realizing my prayers are answered. It is so.

How to Forgive

—�֍.✦—

Forgiveness must take place within your heart and mind to be the real thing. *To forgive* means "to give for." Give yourself the feeling of love and good will instead of the mood of anger, resentment, or hatred. Your mental attitude governs your experience. Keep your mind clear, poised, serene, calm, and full of an expectancy of the best. If you resent another, you are giving too much power to that other and hurting yourself. *To forgive* is to change your thought, and keep it changed. Use the following technique in forgiving another: Whole-heartedly, sincerely, and lovingly pray for the other mentioning his name. Pray: "God is prospering him. The Peace of God fills his soul; he is inspired and blessed in all ways." You rejoice that the Law of God is working for him, through him, and all around him. Do this until your heart and mind are so full of love, there is no room for resentment. You are now free.

Group Healing Prayer

—✖.✦—

We are gathered together in the Presence of God. There is but One God, One Life, One Law, One Mind, and One Father—Our Father. We are all brothers and sisters as we have a common Father.

I salute the Divinity in each person here this morning. The Love of God flows through me to all those present here and to all people everywhere. I believe and know that the Omnipresent Power and Intelligence of the Infinite One moves through every individual here, and that he is positively, definitely, physically, and mentally healed. I know Divine Right Action is taking place in every cell, organ, tissue, and function of each person manifesting as peace, harmony, and health.

I believe that Divine Guidance is being now experienced by every one in this congregation. God—the Great Counselor—leads each of us to ways of pleasantness and paths of peace.

The words which I speak now shall accomplish what I please and prosper whereunto they are sent. I rejoice now and enter into the mood of thankfulness knowing my prayer of faith is fulfilled.

Be Still and Know

Be still and know that I am God. I now still the wheels of my mind as I think of God and His Love. My emotions are controlled perfectly; I am serenely calm. My mind is at peace and it reflects God's Heavenly Truths and Light. The Wisdom of God rises to my surface mind as I am still and calm, revealing to me the perfect plan, showing me the way I should go.

My devotion and attention are focused on God's Eternal Verities all day long. I constantly claim that God's Wisdom, Truth, and Beauty rule and guide me in all phases of my life.

God's rod (Love) and staff (Truth) sustain, nourish, and strengthen me in all endeavors. Whenever fear comes, I immediately turn to God and His Holy Presence rejoicing in this Truth: "God hath not given me the spirit of fear, but of Love, and Power, and a sound mind." I eat of the bread of heaven, made of peace, harmony, and faith in God. My prayer is, "Lord, evermore give us this bread."

Drive In Peace

⊰•⊱

This is God's car. It is God's idea, and it moves from point to point freely, joyously, and lovingly. God's Wisdom guides this car in all its ways. God's Order, Symmetry, and Beauty govern the mechanism of this car at all times. God's Holy Presence blesses this car and all its occupants. The driver of this car is an ambassador of God; he is full of love and good will to all. God's Peace, Truth, and Understanding always govern the driver. God directs all decisions, making straight, beautiful, and perfect the way. The Spirit of the Lord-God is upon the driver, making all roads a highway for his God.

Seaman's Version of the 23rd Psalm

⊰•⊱

The Lord is my Pilot; I shall not drift. He lighteth me across the dark waters; He steereth me in the deep channels; He keepeth my log. He guideth me by the star of holiness for His name's sake. Yea, though I sail 'mid the thunders and tempests of life, I shall dread no danger; for Thou art with me. Thy love and thy care they shelter me. Thou preparest a harbor before me in the homeland of eternity; Thou anointest the waves with oil; my ship rideth calmly. Surely, sunlight and starlight shall favor me on the voyage I take, and I will rest in the port of my God forever."*

---

* (By J. Rogers, a merchant marine captain, written during World War II.) Published by Navy Chaplains Bulletin, Washington, D. C.

King's High Way

ズ・☆

W e will go by the king's highway, we will not turn to the right hand nor to the left."

My way is God's way, and all His ways are pleasantness and all his paths are peace. I travel under God's Guidance led by the Holy Spirit. My highway is the Royal Road of the Ancients, the middle path of Buddha, the strait and narrow gate of Jesus. My highway is the King's Highway, for I am a King over all my thoughts, feelings, and emotions.

I send my messengers called God's Love, Peace, Light, and Beauty before me to make straight, beautiful, joyous, and happy my way. I always travel the King's Highway meeting God's messengers of peace and joy wherever I go. I go by the mountain-top road, knowing that with mine eyes stayed on God, there is no evil on my pathway.

Whilst driving a car, riding on a train, bus, airplane, or on foot, God's Spell is always around me. It is the Invisible Armor of God, and I go from point to point freely, joyously, and lovingly. The Spirit of the Lord, my God, is upon me, making all roads a Highway for my God. It is wonderful!

Prayer for Driving and Traveling

ズ・☆

A nd the Lord, He it is that doth go before thee." My Dominant mood of faith and confidence is that God's Wisdom and Power always rule, guide, and govern me in all ways. This feeling is the Lord that goes before me. My conviction of God's Presence is strong and mighty, and I know the Spiritual atmosphere in which I dwell goes before me, making straight, beautiful, joyous, and happy my way. I know that whenever I travel by bus, train, airplane, automobile, or whatever means of conveyance I use, God's Love and Intelligence guide and govern my journey. All the highways and byways of my world are controlled by God, making the skies above and the earth beneath a highway for my God.

Perfect Eyesight

My eyes are God's eyes, and I see perfectly. The Living Intelligence which made my eyes is now controlling the processes and function of my eyes and my entire body. I know and believe that my vision is Spiritual, eternal, and indestructible. "If, therefore thine eye be single, thy whole body shall be full of Light." This means I see only the Truth; I love the Truth; I know the Truth. I see God in all men and in all things. I see Spiritually, mentally, and physically. My eyes reflect the Glory, Beauty, and the Perfection of God. It is God looking out through my eyes seeing His own ideas of Perfection. My eyes are the windows of my soul; they are pure and are kept single to Love, Truth, and Beauty at all times. The Harmonizing, Healing, Vitalizing, Energizing Power of the Holy Spirit permeates every atom, cell, nerve, tissue, and muscle of my eyes making them whole, pure, and perfect. The Divine, perfect pattern is now made manifest in my eyes, and every atom and cell conform to God's perfect pattern on the Mount. Thank you Father.

His Holy Presence

I am God, and there is no God beside me. I am checked by neither time nor space. I am held by no bonds of name or form. I am present everywhere. I am thy God and Lord of countless hosts. I am in the Holy of Holies, in the Heart of the True Temple on the Holy Mountain. I commune with God now. His Love and Light flow through me, and I am flooded by the Radiance of the Light Limitless. I am lifted up and inspired; I am expanding into the Divine Bosom of the Father. I smell the Sweet Fragrance of God; this Inner Perfume touches my heart strings; it beats to the Melody of God. I place my faith in the Divine Presence and Perfection of He Who Is. My Higher Self is God; He communicates to me; I hear the Inner Voice. It illumines, inspires, and elevates me; periodically, I find myself in ecstasy, immersed in His Holy Omnipresence. Now I know I am a son of the Living God. I am Divine Spirit—a child of God; in Him I live, move, and have my being. I know He is meditating and I am His meditation.

Love's Healing Balm

By this shall all men know that ye are my disciples, if ye love one another." God is the Absolute Lover; hence it follows that before the appeal is made, the answer is given. The Love of God flows through me now; I am surrounded by the Peace of God; all is well. Divine Love surrounds, enfolds, and encompasses me. This Infinite Love is inscribed in my heart and written in my inward parts. I radiate love in thought, words, and deeds. Love unifies and harmonizes all the powers, attributes, and qualities of God within me. Love means joy, peace, freedom, bliss, and praise. Love is freedom. It opens prison doors and sets free all the captives. I am radiating love towards all, for everyone represents the Love of God. I salute the Divinity in the other. I know and believe that Divine Love heals me now. Love is a guiding principle in me; it brings into my experience perfect, harmonious relationships. God is Love. "He that dwelleth in love, dwelleth in God, and God in him."

The Power of God

God is the only Presence and the only Power, and I am one with It. God's Strength is my strength; His Intelligence floods my mind. This new awareness gives me complete dominion in every department of my life. I am now joined to the One Universal Mind. His Wisdom, Power, and Glory flow through me. I know that the Energy and Power of God permeate every atom, tissue, muscle, and bone of my being, making me perfect now. God is Life and this Life is my life. My faith is renewed; my vitality is restored. God walks and talks in me. He is my God; I am one with Him. The Truth is my shield and buckler; I rejoice that it is so. Under His Wings shall I trust. I dwell in the Secret Place of the Most High and I abide under the Shadow of the Almighty.

The Peace of God

A nd into whatsoever house ye enter, first say, Peace be to this house." My mind is flooded with the Life, Love, and Truth of God. Whenever my attention wanders away from God, I bring it back to the contemplation of His Holy Presence. I enter into the Secret Chamber within me—my own consciousness. I am in Heaven; I am perfectly quiet, calm, serene, and poised. "Peace be within thy walls, and prosperity within thy palaces. For my brethren and companion's sakes, I will say, Peace be within thee." I live in the House of the Lord, my God, and I seek only the good. I am living in His Kingdom. I feel and sense the Divine atmosphere of peace, love, and joy. I stir up the gift of God within me. I know that I and my Father are one; I sense and feel the reality of this; His Life flows through me. I know that in His Heaven, where I live, move, and have my being, all my prayers are answered. I am at peace. The Dove of Love has whispered in my ear, "Peace be still!"

My Inner Peace

M y mind is still and at peace; I reflect the Wisdom and Beauty from on High. The Spirit of God flows through me now in thought, word, and deed; I am at peace. The peace that passeth understanding fills me. I sense and feel the security and tranquillity of my mind, which is in tune with the Infinite. I rest in the Everlasting Arms. My life is God's Life, and It is perfect. I am one with my Father, and my Father is God. Poise, balance, and equilibrium are mine now. My mind is God's mind, and it is perfect. God's ideas constantly unfold within me, bringing about harmony, health, and peace. I know the Spirit of Truth is leading me into all Truth. I am poised in the knowledge that God is, and all there is, is God. I radiate the sunshine of God's Love. Love is the fulfilling of the law, and the law is I am that which I contemplate.

Letting Go

I now relax and let go. I am at peace. The peace that passeth understanding fills my mind. There is peace in my home, my heart, and in all my affairs. I let go completely because I know there is a Power responding to me as I speak. This Power flows through me; it vitalizes every atom of my being. I radiate good will to all mankind. My thoughts are God's thoughts, and God's Power is in my thoughts of good. "Be still, and know that I am God." I am still and quiet now because I realize and know that the only Presence and the only Power indwells me. It flows in my behalf; I am at peace, and all is well. Peace, be still. I see the Truth; I love the Truth; I know the Truth. I know that in peace and in confidence lies my strength. His Life, Love, and Truth flow through me now, and I give thanks that "It is done."

Poise and Balance

My mind is full of peace, poise, balance, and equilibrium. There is a deep, inner serenity within me. I am calm now;

I am filled with a sense of peace and Divine justice. There is a Divine solution to all my problems; I give thanks. I dwell in the Secret Place of the Most High and I abide under the Shadow of the Almighty. He is my Refuge and my Salvation. "My God; in Him will I trust." I rejoice in receiving the ideas of God; I am at peace. I know that Infinite Intelligence leads and guides me in all ways. "The sons of God shouted for joy." I am a son of the Living God, and all that the Father hath is mine. I know the Truth; I love the Truth, and I rejoice in the Truth. The Spirit of Truth leads me now into all Truth. I am always thinking rightly. I reflect Divine Wisdom and Divine Intelligence. "With mine eyes stayed on thee, there is no evil on my pathway." My eyes are on the good, and all good is mine. I hear the voice of God; I am at peace.

A Spiritual Treatment

All is Spirit and the manifestation of Spirit. My life is God's Life; I am perfect now. All my organs are God's ideas, which minister and benefit me. I am a spiritual being: I am a perfect reflection of the Perfect God. I feel and know that I am perfect in all ways; I am Spiritual, Divine, and Holy. I am one with my Father, and my Father is God. I am expressing harmony, peace, and joy. All growth in my body and affairs is governed by Infinite Intelligence which is the Active, All-Wise, Law-Abiding Principle called God. I know that I am immersed in the Holy Omnipresence, and every atom, tissue, muscle, and bone of my being are flooded with the Radiance of the Light Limitless. My body is God's body; I am whole and perfect. I am one with God. My mind is flooded with the peace that passeth understanding, and all is well. I thank thee, Father.

Speaking the Truth

—>·<—

I realize and know that when I speak, it is God speaking through me. God speaks by means of man. My words are "apples of gold in pictures of silver." "My words are spirit and they are life. My words are spirit and they are truth." I know the Truth, and the Truth sets me free. My words are full of life, love, and feeling. When I speak, I give joy and happiness to all. I am a messenger of God; I bring glad tidings to all; I speak in peace. God's ideas constantly unfold within me, and they bring harmony, joy, and peace to me. I express myself powerfully and confidently. I am the perfect articulation and expression of Truth. I speak the Truth, love the Truth, and know the Truth. Infinite Intelligence speaks through me now. I now decree a thing, and it shall come to pass. Thank you, Father.

Spiritual Medicine

—>·<—

A merry heart doeth good like a medicine, but a broken Spirit drieth the bones." I am ever joyous, active, and energetic. I am always passing on God's ideas to my fellow man and I give him peace, joy, and happiness. "In thy presence is fullness of joy; at thy right hand there are pleasures for evermore." "The joy of the Lord, is my strength." I am always cheerful, free, and full of happiness. I have dominion over all things in my world; I sense and feel my oneness with God, with life, the universe, and all things. I am perfectly adjusted emotionally. I meditate on whatsoever things are lovely, good, wonderful, and Godlike. The Peace of God is mine now, and I stir up the gift of God which is joy. I am a son of the living God, and "all the sons of God shouted for joy!"

My Faith Makes Me Whole

꧁·꧂

I am spiritual. I am faithful to God or Good. I love only the Good. I am the consciousness of God and reflect His wholeness, completeness, and perfection. I reflect the Perfection of God in every atom of my being. My heart is merry; it maketh a cheerful countenance. My body is God's body; it is perfect now. I am expressing harmony, health, and peace in all the departments of my life. The Light of God shines through my eyes; I see the Truth perfectly. My life is God's life; it is perfect now. It flows through me joyously, harmoniously, and peacefully. The Love of God wells up within me; I express perfect health. I am full of joy and happiness; I am full of confidence and faith. My faith is my inner feeling and conviction that I am whole and perfect. God is the Eternal Now; my good is right this moment. My faith hath made me whole.

Faith In God

꧁·꧂

Jesus said, "Thy faith hath made thee whole." My faith is my inner feeling and conviction that God is, and all there is, is God. I have a joyous expectancy of the best; I know only good can come to me. "Faith is the substance of things hoped for, the evidence of things not seen." Even though I do not see what I want, I know that all things come forth from the Self-Originating Spirit within me. I now turn to God; I think of His qualities, attributes, and aspects. I realize that all these qualities are within me. As I contemplate His Presence, I know peace, order, joy, love, perfection, purity, and holiness flow through my mind and body now. I rejoice in this realization and I give thanks that it is so. I sense and feel my oneness with God, with life, with the universe, and with all men. My faith is in the Law of Good. Right is might. Yes, the right use of the Law of Good or God is mighty over all. I now call things that be not as though they were, and the unseen becomes seen.

Your Health

—◆·◆—

God walks and talks in me. He is my God and He is Perfect. The Spirit within me is ever Perfect, Whole, Happy, and Complete in Itself. I now reflect the Glory and Beauty of the Perfect God. The Light of the One Who Forever Is shines through me and all around me; every atom of my being dances to the rhythm of the Eternal God. My heart is merry; it maketh a cheerful countenance. My words are as a honeycomb; they are sweet to my soul and health to my bones. The Light of God shines out through my eyes; the Love of God wells up in my heart. I know that I do all things through Christ which strengtheneth me. My body is God's body; it is perfect now. The Divine Self within me—right this moment—gives me perfect health, happiness, and harmony. God keeps me in perfect peace. "Father, I thank thee that thou hast heard me. And I knew that thou hearest me always."

Overcome Doubt

I know the Truth which sets me free. God is the Truth, and I am expressing God in all ways. I do not doubt my relatives or friends. Each one of them is expressing God now; I see the Christ in all of them. I give them freedom because I know all belong to God. Divine Love in me causes me to know that I shall receive nothing but Divine Love. I trust my friends, since I trust the God in them. I put away all sense of selfishness and possessiveness. I know Divine Love in me sees the Divine Love in my friends. I salute the Divinity in the other; I am at peace. I know and understand the Truth of Being. I believe only in good. There is nothing but God and His world. I am governed by God. All around me are perfect, spiritual, Divine beings. I love to work with others. I love to represent and express God's ideas; I rejoice in receiving God's ideas in exchange. I am full of joy and happiness, for I am the infinite joy of God. All my fellow-workers are my brothers and sisters. I bless them all. I know they are prospered in all ways. I am full of confidence and faith.

Cast Out Fear

I have absolute trust in God; I expect the best; I know only good can come to me. Divine Love in me casts out all fear; I am at peace. I see the Presence of God everywhere; I am absolutely fearless; God is with me always. If God be for me, who can be against me? I know that one with God is a majority; this heals and frees me from all sense of fear. Only God's thoughts come to me; these thoughts continually unfold, bringing me harmony, joy, peace, and success. I am the consciousness of God; I am surrounded by Divine Love. I think rightly on all occasions. God's Power is with my thoughts of good. His Love. Life, and Truth flow through me; I am immersed in His Holy Omnipresence. I am always surrounded by the Infinite Peace of God. I am full of Divine Understanding. Divine Love goes before me to make straight, perfect, and joyous my way. God walks and talks in me; I know I am one with my Father; my Father is God. I have faith in God; therefore, I fear not. "Fear not, little flock; for it is your Father's good pleasure to give you the Kingdom."

Overcome Resentment

I know that all men are my brothers. All of us have a common Father. I see the Living Christ in everyone I meet. I salute the Divinity in each person. The Love of God flows through me to all mankind. I bless all those who criticize me. I pray for those who speak ill of me. I rejoice to see others succeed. I loose everyone now and I let them go in peace. I open the windows of my mind; I let in the influx of the Holy Spirit. I am perfect and cleansed. I am at peace. The Love of God fills my mind; all is well. I reflect the Love of God; I am absolutely loving toward all. I am conscious of God everywhere because God is over all, through all. I know that the action of God is taking place in the mind and hearts of all. It is wonderful!

Overcome Grief

Man is spiritual and he lives forever. There is no death; all is Life. God is Life and that Life is my life now. I cannot lose that Life. I cease now to grieve over loved ones, for I know they live forever. Where God is, there is no evil; there is only God. I am not separated from loved ones because there is only one Mind and one God. In Him we live, move, and have our being. We are all expressions of the one Being—the one Consciousness. I am instantly in touch with my loved ones, for Spirit is Omnipresent. Every idea that comes to me is from God; these ideas reflect His Beauty and Truth, and they make me absolutely joyous. "The sons of God shouted for joy." I rejoice now to receive God's Truth. "In thy Presence is fullness of joy." Only God's ideas come to me and to my loved ones; all is well.

Overcome Confusion

I know that all things are made by the self-contemplation of Spirit. I am at peace. Peace is the Power at the heart of God. The Self of me is the Living Spirit Almighty. I am full of infinite potentialities. The God-Self fills my mind now with ideas of beauty, perfection, and poise. I have the key to happiness and growth. I am the temple of God; the Spirit of God dwelleth in me. I am never confused because God's ideas unfold in my mind with perfect sequence. All of God's ideas are always available to me; they minister to me and heal me. I am Divinely inspired; my only thoughts are God's thoughts which are perfect, whole, and beautiful. My mind is full of poise, balance, and equilibrium. My mind is the Mind of God. The ideas of God give me joy, happiness, peace, and harmony. "In Thy Presence there is fullness of joy."

True Friendship

≈·≈

I have found my Divine Companion, and He is God. He is fixed in my heart. He walks with me; He talks with me; He tells me I am His own. It is wonderful! I have found my Spiritual friends within; their names are love, joy, peace, gentleness, goodness, faith, meekness, and temperance. These are the only important friends. They are the veritable Almighty Power of God walking in my form. Having found the companions within, I now attract by an Immutable Law people who blend with me spiritually. I radiate friendship and love to the whole, wide world, and to all mankind! I love, and I am loved by everyone. I love people; I am interested in their welfare and happiness. I realize all men are my brothers, and all women are my sisters. I give the best in me to people; they in turn find enjoyment and pleasure in my presence and company. I am now attracting wonderful friends by the Universal Law of Love; God is love. I kiss God now in a mental embrace, for He is my Beloved.

My Divine Companion

I and my Father are one. I know that God is the very life of me. I feel secure now, for I know that Life, Love, and Truth are all within me. I am never alone; God is always with me; "His rod and His staff comfort me." This Inner Presence, the God-Self in me, walks and talks in me. Having found my True and Everlasting Companion within me, I can never lack for wonderful companions in the without. God is the Fullness of all things. My Divine Friend is closer than breathing; He is nearer than hands and feet. I radiate love and friendship to the whole, wide world, and the world responds in kind. I am loving; I am kind. I have a wonderful companion now. This companion blends with me spiritually, mentally, and in all ways. It is wonderful! The Love of God flows through my thoughts, words, and deeds. As within, so without. I have found my Divine Companion within and I now recognize him on the without.

Buying And Selling

I am aware that there is a perfect law of supply and demand. I practice the golden rule in all my affairs. I am at peace. Whatever I wish to sell is an idea in the Mind of God. The Principle of All Knowledge is within me. I know everything that I need instantly. I recognize whatever I wish to buy or sell represents an exchange of ideas in Divine Mind within me. I know there is mutual satisfaction, harmony, and peace. The price is right; the people are right;

all is in perfect order. I know the Truth; I understand the Truth, and I am the consciousness of God in action. All the ideas I need constantly unfold within me with perfect sequence and perfect combinations. I receive and rejoice in Divine ideas and I give them to my fellow creature; I receive ideas in exchange. Peace is mine now. There is no delay in Divine Mind; I accept my good.

Money—God's Idea

❧·❧

I know that money is an idea in Divine Mind. It symbolizes wealth; I recognize it as a means of exchange. All God's ideas are good. God created all things; He pronounced His creation good and very good. Money is good; I use it wisely, judiciously, and constructively. I use it to bless mankind. It is a very convenient symbol; I rejoice in its circulation. God's ideas are instantly available whenever I need them. Money is always available to me; I have a Divine surplus. God is my source of supply; that is my supply now; wealth of all kinds flows to me in avalanches of abundance. There is only One God and One Mind; every idea in the Mind of God is Spiritual. My relationship to money is friendly. It is a symbol of God's Wealth and His Infinite Abundance. The idea of money is omnipresent; I am one with all of the wealth in the world. I use it for good only and I thank thee, Father, for Thy supply.

Wealth Is Mine

❧

God is my source of supply, and I am one with this Infinite sup-ply. All my needs are instantaneously met at every moment of time and point of space. I demonstrate abundance now in all my affairs. I am an inlet and an outlet to the Mind of God. I am fear-less and free. I claim and feel the Spirit of prosperity. I gladly and lovingly serve my fellow man; I attract all good by an Immutable Law of attraction. There is no want, for God is the Source of all. I have instantly everything I need, since I am a Spiritual being. I am governed and supplied by God. I now bring all my empty vessels to the Infinite Storehouse within; the God-Self fills them all; there is a Divine surplus. The Divine Law responds to my faith; my faith and trust is in God, and it is well founded.

Divine Guidance

❧

All things that exist are as a ripple on the surface of the stream and all are of One Substance. All of us share in the quality of the Stream Itself, which is the mirror of myself to myself. "There is a river, the streams whereof shall make glad the city of God." I am the river of God; from me flow forth goodness, truth, and beauty. I dwell in a city of peace; this city is my own mind; all the people, which are my own thoughts, that dwell therein are God's people because they are God's Thoughts, and God's Power is with my thought of good. Infinite Intelligence is guiding me now in thought, word, and deed. I am a perfect channel of the Divine. I feel, know, and believe that my God-Self illumines my pathway. Divine Wisdom inspires, guides, governs, and directs me into all Truth. I am one with God now; all is well. I love the Voice of the Holy One within; it is the voice of my Father, and my Father is God.

How to Realize My Desire

My desire is the Voice of God speaking to me. It is the murmuring and the whispering of my heart. I know that all things are possible with God. God is my Deep-Self—the Formless, Invisible Spirit within me. Being aware of the desire, I know it must exist in the Invisible for me. I know it is mine right this moment. I accept it in my own consciousness. I know that I now have released my desire into the Creative Law, which is the Source of all creation. The Creative Law is within me; it is my own subconscious mind. I know when the idea or desire of mine is impressed in the subjective medium, it must be expressed. I know that feeling is the law, and the law is the feeling. I feel that I am now what I long to be. As I now contemplate my desire, I get the reaction which satisfies. I rejoice in the sense of possession. My whole being thrills to the reality of the fulfilled desire. I am at peace; I rejoice and give thanks, "It is done."

True Place

My work is perfect, and I am always representing God's ideas. I am the consciousness of God; my mind is God's mind. I am the activity of God; I am expressing myself fully. I know there is a perfect law of supply and demand. I am instantly in touch with everything I need. I am in my true place now; I am giving of my talents in a wonderful way. I am Divinely compensated. My God is the Principle of all Knowledge; I know everything that I need instantly. I am one with my Father, and my Father is God. I am always reflecting the Glory, the Love, and the Activity of God. I am doing the thing I love to do. My place is with God at all times; I am one with Him now; it is so. I enter into the joy of it all. I thank you, Father, for my perfect place. All is well.

The Power to Accomplish

For with God nothing shall be impossible." Omnipotence is within me; I am one with all the Power there is. All Truth is the Word of God. I speak the Truth; I rejoice in the Truth. I acknowledge Him; my mind is stayed on Him. I feel the Almighty Power flowing through me now, making me whole and perfect. I reflect Life; I have all power and strength. The joy of the Lord is my strength. I am now individualizing the Infinite Power of His Infinite Love. I express the inexhaustible energy of God. All is Spirit and the manifestation of Spirit. Thine, O Lord, is the Greatness, the Power, the Glory, the Victory, and the Majesty. I am strong in the Lord and in the Power of His Might. The Action of God is taking place in all my affairs; this is the Principle of Good. I know and believe that the Everlasting God in me is the Creator of the ends of the earth. He fainteth not, neither is He weary. I acknowledge this One Power; I consciously unite with It. I rejoice that I am made perfect.

Ability to Achieve

❧·❧

I know instantly everything I need to know, for Infinite Intelligence leads and guides me in all ways. I am the consciousness of God in action. I have absolute trust in this God-Power within me. The right ideas continually unfold in me in perfect sequence and with unfailing regularity. I am inspired from On High; I am forever mounting upward and onward. I am continually with thee. "In thy presence is fullness of joy; at thy right hand there are pleasures for evermore." I am ever joyous. I have the ability and the power to achieve. Whatever I conceive, I can give it conception. I am the activity of God, and that activity is always good. I am always passing on God's ideas to my fellowman, giving him joy and happiness. I am now expressing and manifesting the Light, which is God. I am always alert, alive, and happy. Thank you, Father!

Rising Higher

❧·❧

There is no fear in Love. "Perfect Love casteth out fear." I now possess a deep, inner understanding which makes me master

of all the circumstances of my life. I am in the place of dominion now. I contemplate the Divine Presence within me; I realize
His Life, Love, and Joy flow through me. There is a new buoyancy
in my step; there is a new light in my eyes. I am illumined by the
Light of the One Who Forever Is. I am abiding in Love. I am lifted
up into a higher level of consciousness; I sense the Inner Beau-
ties and Glories of God within. Today I let Love keep me in peace
and harmony. I feel the rhythm of the universe; every atom of my
being dances to the rhythm of the Eternal God. My vision is on
Light, Love, and Truth; I am Divinely led in all ways. My eyes are
on God, and my perception is perfect now. I see God everywhere.
"Lo, I come, and I will dwell in the midst of thee, saith the Lord."

Law of Success

I am the consciousness of God in action. I know it is God working
through me, for God works by means of man. "The Law of the
Lord is perfect." There is a perfect outcome to all my activity. My
work is always successful because it is God's work, which is perfect
and divine. I have instantly everything I need because I am supplied and governed by God. I always know how to obtain everything I need. "My God shall supply all your need according to
his riches in glory." I am full of peace, harmony, and joy. I radiate
Divine Love to all mankind. I am now identified with success; I am
attracting to myself according to an Immutable Law the circumstances, conditions, ideas, finances, and all things necessary for
the unfoldment of my plans. I am Divinely led in all ways. God is
prospering me in mind, body, and affairs. I go to sleep every night
feeling successful and happy. "God giveth to his beloved in sleep."
Thank you, Father.

The Progressive Spirit

—❧•❧—

"They that worship Him must worship Him in spirit and in truth." I now contemplate the fact that Infinite Intelligence dwells within me. There is a Universal Goodness, which is everywhere active and present: I am one with God, with life, the universe, and with all things. The Action of God is taking place now in all my affairs. I am prospered in mind, body, and affairs. I understand the Law of Life is one of progression; I am growing Spiritually in a wonderful way. I am in tune with the Infinite, and God is my Partner. Success is mine now, for I am identified with success and prosperity. I rejoice to see all men grow righteously. I rejoice in the success of all. The Spirit of good will flows from me to all mankind. I am full of confidence and peace. I am illumined by the Light within me. Divine Understanding is a lamp unto my feet, and underneath are the Everlasting Arms.

Eyes and Ears

—❧•❧—

I am the Lord that healeth me. My vision is spiritual, eternal, and a quality of my consciousness. My eyes are divine ideas and they are always functioning perfectly. My perception of spiritual Truth is clear and powerful. The light of understanding dawns in me; I see more and more of God's Truth every day. I see spiritually; I see mentally; I see physically. I see images of Truth and Beauty everywhere.

The Infinite Healing Presence is now, this moment, rebuilding my eyes. They are perfect, divine instruments enabling me to receive messages from the world within and the world without. The Glory of God is revealed in my eyes.

I hear the Truth; I love the Truth; I know the truth. My ears are God's perfect ideas functioning perfectly at all times. My ears are the perfect instruments which reveal God's Harmony to me. The Love, Beauty, and Harmony of God flow through my eyes and ears; I am in tune with the Infinite. I hear the Still, Small Voice of God within me. The Holy Spirit quickens my hearing, and my ears are open and free.

The Power of God

>·<

The Uplifting, Healing, Strengthening Power of the Healing Presence is now restoring every organ of my body. God in the midst of me is Mighty to heal, strengthen, purify, vitalize, and make me every whit whole.

I have complete trust in the Holy Spirit, which is the Presence of God in me. I know that this Divine Presence is bringing all my affairs into Divine order. I have "put on the new man, that after God hath created in righteousness and holiness of truth."

I see and know the Life of God is manifesting now in my flesh. I see God in my entire being; I claim that the Harmony of God is now manifesting Itself in me as strength, purity, beauty, wholeness, perfection, and eternal youth.

The rejuvenating Power of the Spirit is now operating in every cell and fiber of my being, making me whole, pure, fresh, and radiant with Divine Life and Wholeness. Every moment of my life I am growing stronger, healthier, happier, and more youthful. The Vitalizing, Tireless Energy of the Life of God is flowing through me now; I feel wonderful.

Your New Awareness

The Lord is my light and my salvation; whom shall I fear?
the Lord is the strength of my life; of whom shall I be afraid?

PSALMS 27:1.

Affirm daily with deep feeling: I have a new, strong conviction of God's Presence which holds me spellbound, entranced, and unmoved, and I feel serene, confident, and unafraid. I know there is nothing to fear—nothing to draw away from for God is all there is and everywhere present. In Him I live, move, and have my being; so I have no fear. God's envelope of Love surrounds me and His Golden River of Peace flows through me; all is well. I am not afraid of people, conditions, events, or circumstances for God is with me. Faith in God fills my soul, and I have no fear. I dwell in the Presence of God now and forevermore, and no fear can touch me. I am not afraid of the future for God is with me. He is my dwelling place, and I am surrounded with the whole armor of God. God created me and He sustains me. God's wisdom leads and guides me; so I cannot err. I now celebrate the New Year (conviction of God's presence) because I know in my heart the great truth, *"Closer is He than breathing, nearer than hands and feet."*

Dwelling With God

I live in a state of consciousness. It is the consciousness of inner peace, joy, harmony, and good will for all men. I know that my real country is not a geographical location. A country is a dwelling place. I dwell in the Secret Place of the Most High; I abide in the Shadow of the Almighty; I walk and talk with God all the days of my life. I know there is only one Divine Family and that is humanity. *Let God arise, and his enemies be scattered.* PSALM 68:1.

I know that my only enemies are fear, ignorance, superstition, compromise, and other false gods. I will not permit these enemies to dwell in my mind. I refuse to give negative thoughts a passport to my mind.

I enthrone God and His Love in my mind. I think, feel, and act from the standpoint of Divine love. I mentally touch the Divine Power now, and It moves in my behalf; I feel invincible. Peace begins with me. I feel God's river of peace flowing through me now.

I claim the love of God permeates the hearts of all men and God and His Wisdom rule, guide, govern me and all men everywhere. God inspires me, our leaders, and the government of all nations to do His will, and His will only. The will of God is harmony, peace, joy, wholeness, beauty, and perfection. It is wonderful!

Disciplining the Mind

She was found with child of the Holy Ghost. MATT. 1:18.

The *Holy Ghost* means the Holy (whole) Spirit or God which is lodged in the unconscious depths of all men. *Joseph* is your choosing, volitional, or conscious mind. *Mary* represents your deeper mind full of the qualities, attributes, and potencies of God. Joseph, the conscious mind, should be a guide and protector for the holy child which child is your awareness of the presence and power of God within you. Your thought is Joseph, and your feeling or emotion is Mary. When these two unite in peace and harmony, your prayer is answered; this is God in action. This is the way your mind works, and knowledge of this is the birth of the Holy Child or Wisdom in you. Practice a harmonious, synchronous, and joyous relationship between your conscious and subconscious mind and you will bring forth health, peace, strength, and security. Enthrone the right idea in your mind; then you will experience in your heart the true feeling. The union of your thought and feeling represents the married pair in you; when they are fused, the third element *peace* (God) enters in, and you experience the joy of the answered prayer. Let your heart become a chalice for God's love and a manger for His birth; as a result you will express and bring forth a child which is God on earth.

The Thankful Heart

"And one of them when he saw that he was healed, turned back, and with a loud voice glorified God. And fell down on his face at his feet giving him thanks." LUKE 17:15, 16.

"Pray without ceasing. In every thing give thanks."
I THESS. 5:17, 18.

I give supreme recognition to the God-Presence within me. I sincerely and honestly give thanks for all the blessings received. I give thanks for all the good in my life; I live in the feeling of grateful rejoicing. My thankful heart strikes the magic of the divine response. Every day of my life I express thanks for my knowledge of the laws of mind and the way of the Spirit. I know that thankfulness is a movement of the heart first which is followed by a movement of the lips. My uplifted heart opens up the treasure-house of Infinity within me and bespeaks my faith in the fulfillment of my prayers. I am truly thankful because I have found God in the midst of me. "I sought the Lord, and He heard me and delivered me from all my fears." He who possesses a thankful heart is always in tune with the Infinite and cannot suppress the joy that arises from contemplating God and His Holy Presence. In everything, give thanks.

Thought Power

-><-

Man is what he thinks all day long. "As a man thinketh in his heart, so is he." Have a healthy regard and a wholesome respect for your thoughts. Your health, happiness, success, and peace of mind are largely determined by your awareness of the power of thought. You have heard it said that thoughts are things, and that thoughts execute themselves. Your thought is a definite force. When you think the thought, you are actually releasing its latent power into action.

Think on whatsoever things are true, lovely, elevating, and Godlike and be absolutely convinced of the supremacy and authority of thought. You must definitely believe in your own thought, not merely as yours, but as a power in its own right; then you will make your prayers effective.

The plant is in the seed. The oak is in the acorn. You don't give the seed vitality; it has its own mathematics, mechanics, and mode of expression; likewise the thought is the power; you do not give it power. Know this and you will be free from strain and anxiety. To think with confidence in the power of your thought is the action of God in you, and "He never faileth."

Move onward and upward by recognizing the supremacy of the Spiritual Power and the authority of your thought. This is the way to get marvelous results. This knowledge augments your faith enabling you to experience the joy of the answered prayer.

Banish Anxiety

❧·❧

The Lord is my light and my salvation;
Whom shall I fear?
The Lord is the strength of my life;
Of whom shall I be afraid?

This one verse of the Twenty-seventh Psalm gives personal freedom from all fear. It reveals to you the source of all power, strength, and wisdom. It enables you to reject the power of externals, takes the burden off your shoulders, and sets you on the high road to peace of mind, health, and happiness.

The Lord is the Presence of God, the I AM within you. In simple, psychological language, the Lord is your consciousness. What is consciousness? Your state of consciousness is the way you think, feel, believe, and the reasoning behind your belief. The cause of all your experiences is your thought and feeling.

Refuse to give power to conditions, circumstances, and the external world. Your thought initiates causation. Your thinking is cause; the condition is not causative. There is no power to challenge Omnipotence; therefore, there is nothing to fear. If fear comes to your mind, go within to your Divine Center; think of God and His Power, realizing there is only One Power, and you are one with It now. In this stillness, nothing external can inhibit, obstruct, or thwart you. Think of new and better conditions, the way you want things to be. Realize that as you think, it is Omnipotence thinking and moving on your behalf. The outcome is sure and certain, for it is God in action.

God is the name for the One Power acting beneficently in your life. This Power is Sovereign, Supreme, One and Indivisible. It is self-moving. This Power inspires you, guides you, watches over you, strengthens you, and protects you in ways you know not of. God lives and reigns in your life. A realization of this truth is your salvation.

A Better Future

God hath not given us the spirit of fear, but of power, and of love, and of a sound mind.

Each day is a time of renewal, resurgence, and rebirth. All nature proclaims the glory of a new day. This is to remind us that we must awaken the God within us and arise from our long winter sleep of limitation and walk forth into the morning of a new day and a new life. Fear, ignorance, and superstition must die in us, and we must resurrect faith, confidence, love, and good will.

Begin now to take the following transfusion of God's grace and love, "I am filled with the freeflowing, cleansing, healing, harmonizing, vitalizing life of the Holy Spirit. My body is the temple of the Living God, and it is pure, whole, and perfect in every part.

Every function of my mind and body is controlled and governed by Divine Wisdom and Divine Order.

I now look forward to a glorious future. I live in the joyous expectancy of the best. All the wonderful God-like thoughts I am thinking now, this day, sink down into the subconscious mind as into a tomb. I know when their time is ready, they will come forth as harmony, health, peace, conditions, experiences, and events.

I now pass over from fear and lack to freedom in God and the abundant life. The God-man is risen in me. Behold! I make all things new!"

The Holy Man
(Adapted from The Holy Shadow)

Long, long ago, there lived a Holy Man so good that the astonished angels came from heaven to see how one could be so godly. He simply went about his daily life radiating love as the star diffuses light and the flowers perfume without even being aware of it. Two words summed up his day: He gave, and he forgave. Yet these words never fell from his lips; they were expressed in his ready smile, his kindness, love, and good will.

The angels said to God, "Oh Lord, grant him the gift of miracles!"

God replied, "I consent; ask what he wishes."

"What do you desire then?" cried the angels.

"What can I wish for?" asked the Holy Man smiling. "That God give me His grace, with that should I not have everything?"

The angels insisted, "You must ask for a miracle, or one will be forced upon you."

"Very well," said the Holy Man, "that I may do a great deal of good without ever knowing it."

The angels were greatly perplexed. They took counsel together and resolved upon the following plan: Every time the Holy Man's shadow should fall behind him, or at either side, so that he could not see it, it should have the power to cure disease, soothe pain, and comfort sorrow.

And so it came to pass. When the Holy Man walked along, his shadow on the ground, on either side or behind him, made arid paths green, caused withered plants to bloom, gave clear water to dried-up brooks, fresh color to pale little children, and joy to unhappy mothers. The Holy Man simply went about his daily life pouring forth love as the star diffuses light and the flower perfume without ever being aware of it.

And the people respecting his humility followed him silently, never speaking about his miracles. Little by little, they came even to forget his name, and called him only, "The Holy Man."

Discovering the Power

❦

You will discover the deep reservoirs of power the moment you assume they are there and act as though you were convinced of that great truth. "He who perseveres to the end shall be saved."

Success, the answer to your prayer, the solution you are seeking come as you keep on keeping on. You never give up; neither do you take "No" for an answer. Keep on moving forward. The athlete who is running in a race ofttimes gets tired, weary, exhausted, and ready to give up. He rejects the thought of failure completely by calling on the God-Power to renew his strength; then a tremendous change takes place. A great wave of strength and vitality moves through him. The psychologist calls it his "second wind."

Don't stop before you get your second wind or you will never discover the Hidden Power. The Power that moves the world is within you. Act as though you believed it is there and you will work miracles in your life, transcending your wildest dreams.

"But they that wait upon the Lord shall renew their strength; they shall mount up with wings as eagles; they shall run, and not be weary; and they shall walk, and not faint." ISA. 40:31.

Let Go and Let God Do It

⇒•⇐

You have been given dominion. You are the master of your thoughts, emotions, and responses to life. Your thought is creative, because your subconscious mind responds to the nature of your thought. When you pray, you must be a very good executive; you must learn to delegate your work wisely and judiciously. God in His Wisdom has given you a subconscious mind which is a wonderful servant. It obeys your command. You are the captain decreeing orders, and your subconscious mind faithfully carries out your decrees. When you have a problem, you turn your request for a solution over to the Deeper Mind which is in touch with Infinite Intelligence and Boundless Wisdom. The Deeper Mind knows how to solve your problem and present you with the answer. Turn your request over now with faith and confidence knowing in your heart you will have actually turned your request over or not by the way you feel inside. If you trust the inner power, you are peaceful and calm. *In quietness and confidence shall be your strength.* Isaiah 30:15.

Words of Power

❧•❧

I stay my mind upon God and I am kept in perfect peace. In this peace of God I find Order, Harmony, and Divine Love.

"No word of God shall be void of power."

The words that I speak are full of spirit and full of life. I acknowledge God in all my affairs and transactions. My mind is stayed on Him. I am blessed and prospered by the activity of the law of good operating in my life.

All my statements of truth are charged with life, love, and meaning. The words I speak make a deep impression on my deeper mind. I am glad I know God dwells in my heart, for God is the very life of me. These words sink into my heart, "Behold, I dwell with thee, O man of God, and thou dwellest with me."

I know that when I look at my fellow man, I am seeing God in human form. I bless and send forth loving thoughts to all mankind. I speak the word now. My words are creative; the deeper mind within me responds. I now decree perfect health, harmony, and peace in my home, my heart, and all my affairs.

I know and believe that God is guiding me now in all my ways, and that Infinite Spirit governs all my actions. I have decreed it; it shall come to pass. I have found the Jewel of Eternity in my own heart.

Prosperity

—⋺·⋵—

Let the words of my mouth, and the meditation of my heart, be acceptable in thy sight, O Lord, my strength, and my redeemer.   PSALM 19:14.

One of the best ways to bring prosperity into your life is to have the thankful heart. Always give thanks, and praise the increase which comes to you.

If you select a rose bush in your garden, and bless it several times a day, it will respond with a lavish blossoming which will exceed all the other roses.

Give thanks by having the grateful and uplifted heart for the wonderful food on the table. You prosper by blessing members of the household and all people everywhere. To bless the other, claim that the Presence of God is in the person, and that he is radiating and expressing more and more of God's Love, Light, and Truth. Bless all of your relatives; bless every situation; bless your home, your environment, your work, and your office. You are actually putting into application one of the great laws of prosperity also.

To prosper means to grow spiritually, mentally, and materially. Claim now: "I am going to put the law of prosperity into operation in a wonderful way in my life!" Do it in this way: Say frequently, "I bless and prosper every member of my family. I give thanks, I praise, and I exalt God in my husband, my wife, and in my children. I bless everything they are doing. I bless all of the gifts I make. I know it is more blessed to give than to receive. I bless my business. I pray for and bless my workers, my customers, and all people. My work prospers, multiplies, increases, and returns to me a thousand fold."

Onward and Upward

Maintain a positive, constructive attitude of mind and you will move onward, upward, and Godward. Sometimes people will tell you about the bad things that are bound to come; it seems that they do not know any reason why something good should happen. They say prayer is a state of wishful thinking. *Wishful thinking* to them means a wish that cannot be realized, or a wish that is too good to be true.

There is not anything too good to be true nor is there anything too wonderful to last. Claim your good now and walk in the assumption that all good things are yours.

Desires knock at the door of every heart. It is the inner voice within all of us which is saying, "Come on up higher!" Prayer is entering into the realization of the wish fulfilled. If wishful thinking is wishing or desiring something without realizing it, let us ask who is the wishful thinker? He is the person who does not understand prayer. He desires health, wealth, prosperity, and true expression, but he says in his heart, "I do not believe; I have no faith." In other words he lacks faith and confidence to which the everlasting principle of life responds in all of us.

The scientific thinker knows there is a way to realize an answer to his desires. He recognizes there is a subjective law within him which responds to his faith and conviction. He realizes if he prays believing, he shall receive. His faith is well founded; he is at peace. Such a person has turned his request over to this other mind knowing it will answer him.

Do not look at the top of the mountain and say, "It is impossible!" You are in Truth. Your vision is on the Summit, and your faith will take you there.

God's Circle of Love

The gifts of God are mine now. I live in the Presence of God from whom all blessings flow. I use every moment of this day to glorify God. God's harmony, peace, and abundance are mine now. Divine love flowing from me blesses all who come into my atmosphere. God's love is felt by all present here, and His love is healing them now.

I fear no evil for God is with me. I am always surrounded by the sacred circle of God's love and power. I claim, feel, know, and believe definitely and positively that the spell of God's love and eternal watchfulness guides, heals, and watches over me and all members of my family.

I forgive everyone, and I sincerely radiate God's love, peace and good will to all men everywhere. At the center of my being is peace; this is the peace of God. In this stillness I feel His strength, guidance, and the love of His Holy Presence. I am divinely guided in all my ways. I am a clear channel for God's love, light, truth, and beauty. I feel His River of Peace flowing through me now. I know that all my problems are dissolved in the mind of God. God's ways are my ways. The words I have spoken accomplish that whereunto they are sent. I rejoice and give thanks realizing my prayers are answered. It is so.

How to Give a Treatment

Spiritual treatment means that you turn to the Indwelling God and remind yourself of His peace, harmony, wholeness, beauty, boundless love, and limitless Power. Know that God loves you and cares for you. As you pray this way the fear will gradually fade away. If you pray for a heart condition, do not think of the organ as diseased as this would not be spiritual thinking. Thoughts are things. Your spiritual thought takes the form of cells, tissues, nerves, and organs. To think of a damaged heart or high blood pressure tends to suggest more of what you already have. Cease dwelling on symptoms, organs, or any part of the body. Turn your mind to God and His love. Feel and know that there is only one healing Presence and Power, and to its corollary: *There is no power to challenge the action of God.*

—o—

Quietly and lovingly affirm that the uplifting, healing, strengthening Power of the healing Presence is flowing through you making you every whit whole. Know and feel that the harmony, beauty, and Life of God manifest in you as strength, peace, vitality, beauty, wholeness, and right action. Get a clear realization of this, and the damaged heart or other diseased condition will dissolve in the Light of God's love.

Glorify God in your Body. I Cor. 6:20.

How to Use the Power of Prayer

*This book consists of ten of the most popular lessons
from Dr. Murphy's radio programs, and is designed
to give you a fundamental, basic, overall grasp of the
essence of practical, mental laws. Each lesson reveals
to you, how you can use the healing power, and
attain the deepest desires of your heart.*

*He is an internationally known author, teacher, and
lecturer. Thousands have heard him lecture and have
been benefited by his tried and tested teachings.*

*Most of the common problems in everyday life he
has had to meet, and now shows you in a simple,
direct manner how you can solve your problems,
and lead a more full, and happy life.*

"He that dwelleth in the secret place of the most High shall abide under the shadow of the Almighty."

Dedicated to:

Robert
who is in favour with God and man.

Contents

1

How Your Mind Heals You

There is a Healing Presence within you which heals all manner of disease. To use this Healing Presence requires knowledge of God, and the way He works.

Spiritual healing refers to wholeness, completeness, and perfection.

Science means knowledge of laws and principles; it means systematized and coordinated knowledge.

Knowledge of this Healing Principle is taken directly from the Bible. The means by which we unlock the mysteries, and reveal the hidden meaning of the Bible from Genesis to Revelation is the science of symbology and the science of the Hebrew alphabet.

The Bible deals with spiritual and mental laws. It recognizes the fact that many of the characters, such as Jesus, Moses, Elijah, Paul, and others were real men who lived on earth; nevertheless, they also represent states of mind within all of us. The Bible is a spiritual and psychological textbook.

Through the study and application of mental laws, *you* can find the way to health, harmony, peace, and prosperity; scientific prayer is the practice of the Presence of God.

Three Steps In Healing

The first step: Think of God as the only Presence and the only Power; God is a universal, creative Spirit present everywhere—the Living Spirit Almighty fixed in your own heart. Dwell on some of the things you know to be true about God; say quietly, for example: "He is Infinite Intelligence, Absolute Goodness, Infinite Power, Indescribable Beauty, Boundless Love, Infinite Wisdom, and All Powerful."

The second step: Forgive everyone; send loving thoughts to the whole world. Say, "I fully and freely forgive *everyone* now, and I go free." Add sincerely from your heart, "I mean this; it is true." You do not have any mental reservations.

The third step: Claim calmly and lovingly that the Infinite Healing Presence of God within you is now healing your body, making it whole, pure, and perfect. Declare to yourself, "I believe this; I accept it; I know the healing is taking place now." Give thanks for the harmony and peace that are yours.

"God in the midst of you is mighty to heal."

2

Practice of the Presence of God

The Omnipresence of God, means that God is present at every moment of time and every point of space. To practice the Presence of God all day long is the key to harmony, health, peace, joy, and a fullness of life. Begin now to see God in everyone and in everything.

The first step: Accept the fact that God is the only Presence and the only Power; He is the very Life and Reality of you.

The second step: Realize the Presence of God in all of the members of your family and in every person you meet. Salute the Divinity from this moment forward in everyone who crosses your path.

The third step: Realize, know, and claim that everything you are and everything you see, whether it is a tree, dog, or cat, is a part of God's expression; this is the greatest thing you can do; it is powerful beyond words.

Sit down quietly two or three times a day, and think along these lines: God is all there is; He is all in all. Begin to realize that the Divine Presence is within you and within everyone around you. *"Seek and you shall find. Seek ye first the Kingdom of God, and his righteousness; and all these things shall be added unto you."*

3

Change Fear To Faith

Whenever fear enters your mind, it is a signal for action; do something about it immediately; never surrender to your fear. Your fear is really a desire for something better; it is a longing for freedom and peace of mind. Where will you get your freedom and peace of mind? You will find it in the thoughts of peace, freedom, and poise.

If a man loses his way in the woods at night, fear seizes him; but knowing that God is all-wise, and knows the way out, he changes from fear to faith. He is now changing from the mood of fear to the mood of confidence and peace in the only Presence and the only Power. He has changed his mental attitude; this is often referred to as the Angel of God's Presence which leads him out into safety. The man who is lost turns to God in prayer and recognition, and says to himself quietly and lovingly, "God is guiding me now. He is a lamp unto my feet." He trusts and believes in this inner Light; this is the Light that lighteth every man that cometh into the world.

One with God is a majority! There is only fear and love. Fear is love in reverse. Love frees; it gives; it is the Spirit of God. Love builds the body. Love is also an emotional attachment. So fall in love with peace, gentleness, success, goodwill, and harmony, for this form of love casts out fear.

"God is love; and he that dwelleth in love dwelleth in God, and God in him."

Three Steps In Banishing Fear

The first step: "THE LORD is my light and my salvation; whom shall I fear? the LORD is the strength of my life; of whom shall I be afraid." *The Lord* means the Presence of God within you. There is no power to challenge God, for God is Almighty. The thing you fear has no power; it is a false belief; it is the bogey man under the stairs, and has no reality. Repeat these wonderful words: "God hath not given us the Spirit of fear; but of power, and of love, and of a sound mind."

The second step: You overcome fear by faith in God and all things good. Faith is not a creed, dogma, or a religion. Faith is a way of thinking; it is a positive, mental attitude. Faith is vital; it is a deep, abiding conviction in God. Faith is the greatest medicine in the world! Take this spiritual medicine of faith now! Look at these words; repeat them: "'I do all things through Christ which strengtheneth me.' God is with me now. God and His Holy Angels are always with me. I am surrounded by the circle of God's Love." These words are now reflected in your brain and deeper mind. Repeat these powerful statements, and all fear will leave you.

The third step: When fear thoughts come, think of God; imagine you are now resting in the arms of Almighty God in the same way as you rested in your loving mother's arms.

Say lovingly to your Father within, "Now, God, I am going about my business, and you are going with me. Your Love, Light, and Power comfort, guide, and bless me in all ways. I love my Father, and my Father loves me; my Father is God! It is wonderful!"

4

Overcome Worry

orry is due to a lack of faith in God. The person who worries is always expecting things to go wrong. They brood or worry over a great many things that never happen. Such a person tells you all of the reasons why something bad should happen, and not one reason why something good should happen. This constant worry debilitates their entire system, resulting in physical and mental disorders.

Your worry can be cured. Do not spend time looking at your troubles or problems; cease all negative thinking. Your mind will not work when it is tense. It relieves the strain to do something soothing and pleasant when you are presented with a problem. You do not fight a problem, but you can overcome it.

To release pressure, take a drive; go for a walk; play solitaire; read a favorite chapter of the Bible, such as: the eleventh chapter of Hebrews, or 1 Corinthians, 13; or turn to the forty-sixth Psalm; read it over carefully and quietly several times. An inner calm will steal over you, and you are ready to pray.

Steps In Overcoming Worry

The first step: Every morning when you awaken turn to God in prayer as you would to your loving Father. Relax the body; then talk to God, the only Presence and the only Power. Become as a little child; this means that you realize God is within you; you trust Him completely. "God in the midst of you is Mighty to heal."

The second step: You know in your heart that you can present your problems or difficulties to this Power, and that the Wisdom of God will solve it for you. Say lovingly: "Thank you, Father, for this wonderful day. It is God's day; it is filled with joy, peace, happiness, and success for me. I look forward with a happy expectancy to this day. The Wisdom and Understanding of God will govern me during the entire day. God is my partner; everything I do will turn out in a wonderful way. I believe in God; I trust God."

The third step: You are full of confidence and faith. Now let go; and let God work through you. Remember as you go through your day: "This is the day God made for me! There is Divine activity taking place in my life."

5

Desire—the Gift of God

God speaks to you through desire. All things begin with desire; it is sometimes called the fountain of all action. As you read this, you have within you the urge or desire to be greater than you are. There is a Cosmic urge within you seeking expression. Life seeks to express its unity, wholeness, love, and beauty through you. You are an instrument of the Divine; you are a channel for Life and Love. You are here to release the imprisoned splendor within you.

Without desire you could not move from your chair. Man desires shelter, and he proceeds to build houses to protect himself from the inclemencies of the season. Man plants seeds of corn and wheat in the ground, because he desires food for his family and himself.

You have a supreme desire now; perhaps it is for health, true place, or abundance. Desire unduly prolonged results in frustration and sickness. To desire something good and wonderful over a long period of time, and not attain it, is to waste away in spirit and body. You should learn to realize your desire through prayer; the realization of your desire is your saviour.

The Three Steps In Realizing Your Desire

The first step: Realizing your desire for harmony, peace, health, true place, wealth, etc., is the voice of God speaking to you. Say from your heart, "With God all things are possible." God is the Living Spirit Almighty within you from which all things flow.

The second step: I am aware of my desire; I know it exists in the Invisible for me. I claim it is mine now; I accept it in my own mind. I have released my desire into the Creative Medium within me, which is the source of all things. I claim and believe that my desire is now impressed in my deeper mind. What is impressed must be expressed; this is the way my mind works.

The third step: I now feel the reality of my fulfilled desire. I am at peace. I know in my heart what I have accepted as true will come to pass. I rejoice and give thanks. My whole being thrills to the reality of the fulfilled desire. I am at peace. God is peace. Thank you, Father, it is done.

6

Happy Marriage

Wat god hath joined together, let no man put asunder." A husband and wife should each be married to God and all things good. A husband and wife should never let the sun go down on their wrath. Never carry over from one day to another accumulated irritations arising from little disagreements. Be sure to forgive each other for any sharpness before you retire at night.

The answer to a happy marriage is for each one to see the Christ in the other; begin now to see the Presence of the Living God in each other. Say to yourself now, "I salute the Divinity in my husband or in my wife," as the case may be. Say to your wife or husband, "I appreciate all you are doing, and I radiate love and goodwill to you all day long." Do not take your marriage partner for granted; show your appreciation and your love.

Think appreciation and goodwill, rather than condemnation, criticism, and nagging. Remember the injunction of the Bible, "Except the Lord build the house, they labor in vain that build it." The way to build a peaceful home and a happy marriage is upon the basis of love, beauty, harmony, mutual respect, faith in God, and in all things good.

Say from your heart, "My marriage is consecrated in prayer and love." A husband and wife should always pray together at least once a day, preferably at night before retiring; this will restore peace in the home and in the heart; for God is peace.

Three Steps to a Happy Marriage

The first step: In the beginning God. The moment you awaken in the morning, claim God is guiding you in all ways. Send out loving thoughts of peace, harmony, and love to your marriage partner, to all members of the family, and to the whole world.

The second step: Say grace at breakfast. Give thanks for the wonderful food, for your abundance, and for all of your blessings. Make sure that no problem, worries, or arguments shall enter into the table conversation; the same applies at dinner time.

The third step: Husband and wife should alternate in praying each night. Keep the Bible close at hand. Read the 23rd, 91st, 27th Psalms, the 11th Chapter, Hebrews, the 13th Chapter, 1 Corinthians, and other great texts of the New Testament before going to sleep. Say quietly, "Thank you, Father, for all the blessings of the day. God giveth his beloved sleep."

7

The Secret of Peace of Mind

Communion with God is the way to peace of mind; this means turning to God in prayer and realizing that His Peace and Love are now flowing through your mind and heart. Prayer, or this silent communion with God within you, will change your character. Prayer makes you a different person.

The word *prayer* may be understood as including any form of communion with God whether vocal or mental. Peace of mind is achieved by getting a real sense of the Presence of God within you. In trying to bring peace into the lives of others, your personal opinion is usually wrong. By interfering in their strife, you usually make matters worse. By getting them to patch up their differences or arriving at a compromise to which they agree, there is no true peace, because they have not completely forgiven each other. The best way to heal quarrels of this nature is the silent way of prayer.

Realize the Wisdom, Love, and Peace of God are flowing through the minds and hearts of all concerned; the trouble will dissolve in a wonderful way. "Blessed are the peace makers; for they shall be called the children of God."

Three Steps to Peace of Mind

The first step: Realize God is Peace, and that He dwells in the midst of you; then think of that inner peace as yours now. Say quietly several times: "The Peace of God that passeth all understanding now floods my mind and heart."

The second step: Know that you have in your mind that which you constantly practice. Say frequently during the day, "I know that peace of mind is mine, because I enthrone thoughts of peace, harmony, and goodwill in my mind; I live with these ideas all day long."

The third step: Read the twenty third Psalm every night; relax the body; say, "I now enthrone in my mind thoughts of peace, love, and goodwill. God is my shepherd, and God's river of peace flows through me now. I lay me down in peace to sleep; for thou LORD, only maketh me dwell in safety."

8

You Can Have a Better Future

Remember what Paul said, "Faith without works is dead." You must demonstrate your faith. Faith is a way of thinking, an attitude of mind, a positive, affirmative approach toward life.

If you live, for example, in the joyous expectancy of the best, invariably the best will come to you.

You are demonstrating to the world that your faith is in all things good.

Live in the firm conviction of your oneness with God, with Life, and with the Universe. You will find yourself attracting to you wonderful people, greater prosperity, and increased awareness of God's Wisdom. Claim every day of your life that Divine Intelligence is directing your footsteps along the right path; know that God is your source of supply; He is the giver of every perfect gift. Realize that all of your needs are met, and that there is a Divine surplus.

To attain peace and harmony, say from your heart every morning as you arise, "God's peace, the peace that passeth all understanding, fills my mind and heart." Paul says that all things work together for good to them that love God. God and good are synonymous. You are in tune with all things Godlike, and behold, "If any man be in Christ, he is a new creature."

Three Steps to a Better Future

The first step: In all thy ways acknowledge Him, and He will make plain thy path, trust also in Him, and believe in Him, and He will bring it to pass. Turn to God within you; claim God is governing all of your affairs.

The second step: Realize the way to get along with people and adjust yourself to life is to love them. Let your heart be motivated by love and goodwill toward all around you. Pray for the peace and prosperity of all of those with whom you are associated.

The third step: Have a definite mental attitude of success. When presented with a problem, realize the Infinite Intelligence of God is revealing to you the perfect plan and showing you the way you should go. As you go to sleep say, "God knows the answer." Feel the joy of the answered prayer.

9

Overcome Irritation

He *whose spirit is without restraint, is like a city that is broken down and without walls." "He that ruleth his spirit is greater than he that taketh a city."*

In order that you might lead a full and happy life, control of the emotions is essential. To govern and control your emotions and temper tantrums, it is essential to maintain control over your thoughts. As a matter of fact you cannot find peace any other way. Will power or mental coercion will not do it. Forcing yourself to suppress your anger is not the way.

The answer is to enthrone God-like thoughts in your mind; busy yourself mentally with the concepts of peace, harmony, and goodwill. Keep firm control over your thoughts. Learn to substitute love for fear, and peace for discord.

You can direct your thoughts along harmonious lines. For example, if you see or hear of something that disturbs or angers you, instead of giving way to anger or irritation, say automatically, "The peace of God that passeth all understanding is now flooding my mind, my body, and my whole being." Repeat this phrase several times during the period of stress; you will find all tension and anger disappear.

Fill your mind with Love, and the negative thoughts cannot enter. When someone says something sharp or critical to you, think on a single statement of Truth, such as, "God is Love. He leadeth me beside the still waters." Peace steals over you; you will radiate this peace.

The Following Three Steps Will Be Found Most Helpful

The first step: As you awaken in the morning, say to yourself: "This is God's day; it is a new day for me, a new beginning. The restoring, healing, soothing, loving power of God is flowing through me, bringing peace to my mind and body now and forevermore."

The second step: Should some business problem or some person upset or irritate you, think immediately about His Holy Presence. Say, "God is with me all day. His peace, His Guidance, and His Love enable me to meet all problems calmly and peacefully."

The third step: Radiate Love to all of your associates. Claim they are doing their best. Say, "I wish them peace, harmony, and joy. I salute the God in them." And lo and behold, God and His Love come forth!

10

Your Spiritual Rebirth

When the storm of life disturbs you, and it appears that your ship is about to founder, remember that it is time for you to awaken to the Christ within. This is how you become reborn spiritually: Recall to mind that God is within you, the very life of you. "Closer is He than breathing, nearer is He than hands and feet." Realize that "With God all things are possible." Claim and know that the God-Power within you is able to cope with any difficulty. Dwell on the peace and harmony of God where the difficulty is, and a perfect, Divine solution will follow.

If troubled say, "Peace be still!" The peace of God will steal over you. Turn your burdens (your problems) over to the God-Wisdom within you, knowing and believing that the perfect solution will come to you in God's own way. When you do this with faith and confidence, the storm or anxiety will pass away, and a great calm will steal over you; this is the peace that passeth all understanding. If you are living in limitation and sickness, this is bondage and restriction; it means you are in the dark as to the higher side of life and your tremendous potentialities. When you catch a glimpse of a higher set of facts, the old way of thinking will be displaced; then your Christ or inner Life will rise from the dead or limited state.

Enthrone the concept of peace, harmony, and success in your mind; busy your mind with these things; you will find your body and circumstances will reflect your inner, mental attitude; this is the new birth of freedom. Remove prejudices, deceit, and jealousies from your mind by opening your mind to the Light of God's Love and inspiration. God's Love revivifies and thrills you; this is the birth of God in you.

Three Steps To Your Spiritual Rebirth

The first step: "I saw a new heaven and a new earth." I know now that God's Love springs in my soul. My heart feels the Presence of God, because I radiate Love and joy to all.

The second step: Any time a negative, fearful, critical thought comes to me, I say, "God is with me." This kills it; then my soul is filled with Love toward all.

The third step: Remember always that God never changes. God is within you—your loving Father—Who is saying, "Fear not, child, for all is thine!"

About the Author

A native of Ireland who resettled in America, Joseph Murphy, Ph.D., D.D. (1898–1981) was a prolific and widely admired New Thought minister and writer, best known for his metaphysical classic, *The Power of Your Subconscious Mind*, an international bestseller since it first appeared on the self-help scene in 1963. A popular speaker, Murphy lectured on both American coasts and in Europe, Asia, and South Africa. His many books and pamphlets on the auto-suggestive and metaphysical faculties of the human mind have entered multiple editions—some of the most poignant of which appear in this volume. Murphy is considered one of the pioneering voices of affirmative-thinking philosophy.

Printed in the USA
CPSIA information can be obtained
at www.ICGtesting.com
JSHW051023230524
R13534700005B/R135347PG63569JSX00008B/3